Vol 11

MAZE

Ages 4-6

FOR KIDS

MAZE BOOK

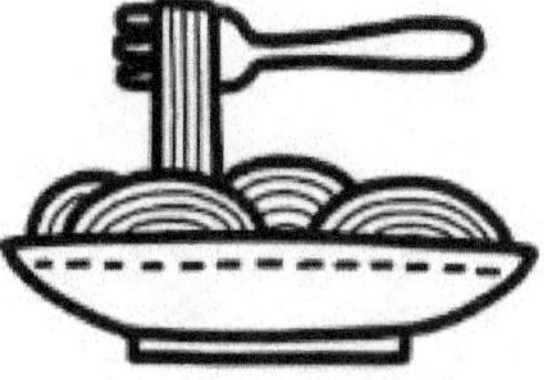

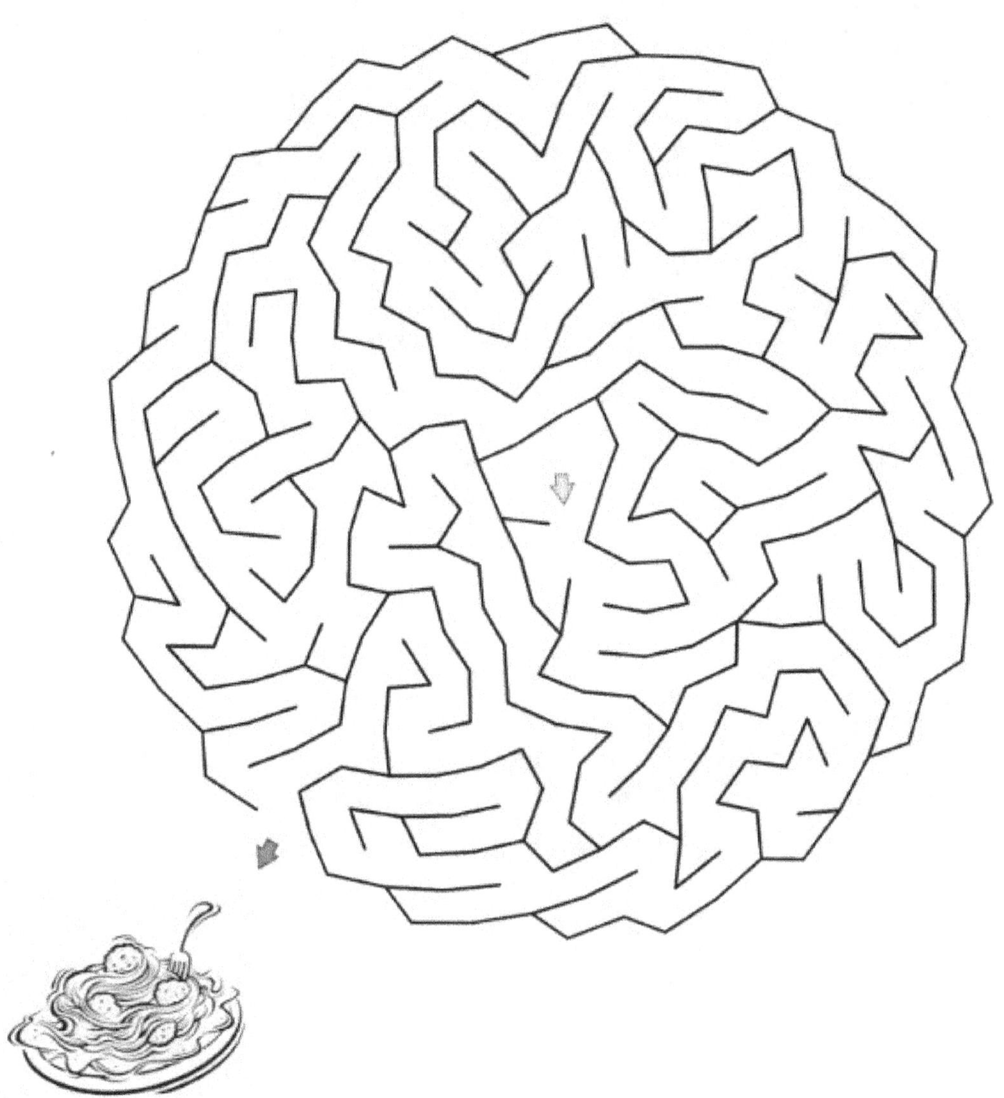

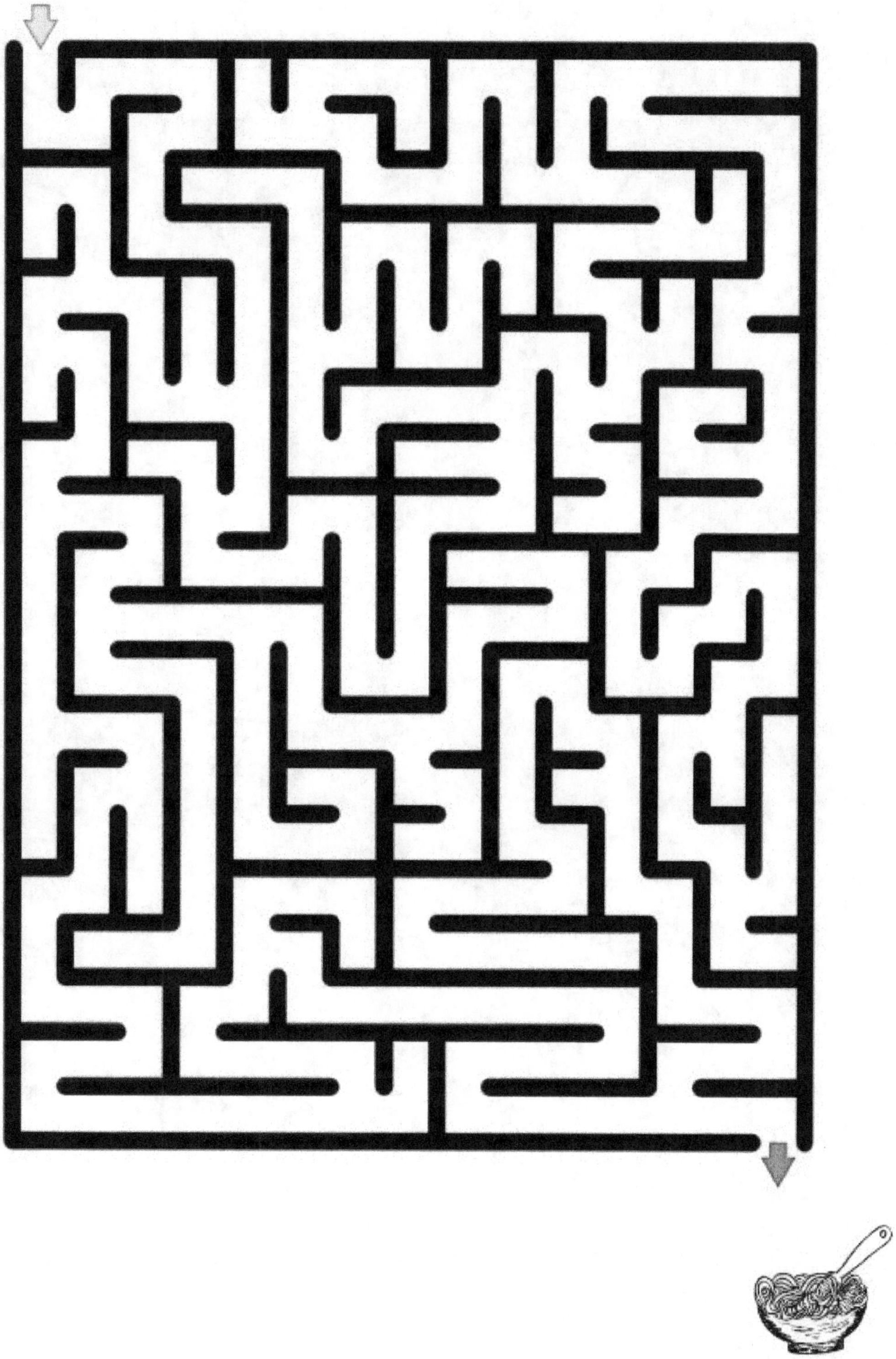

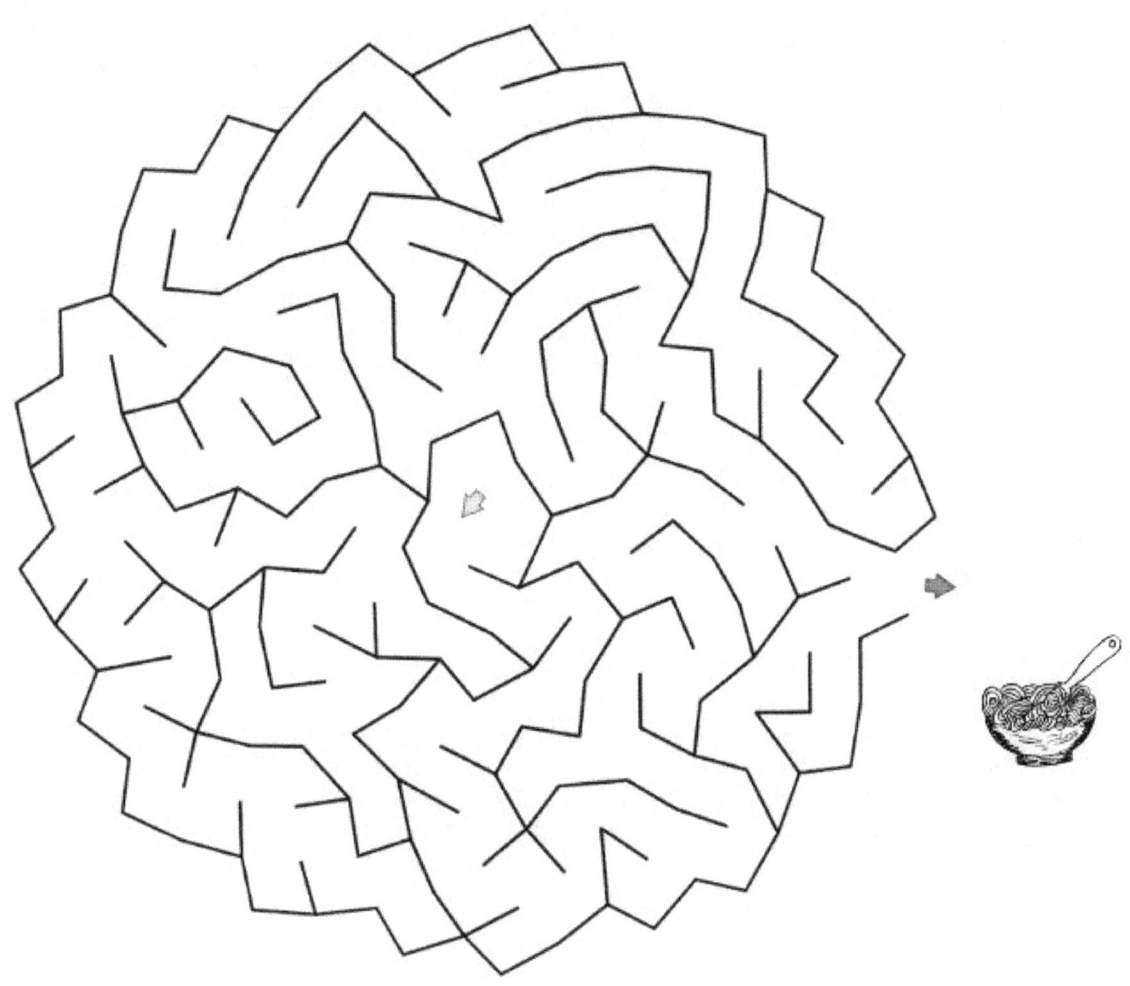

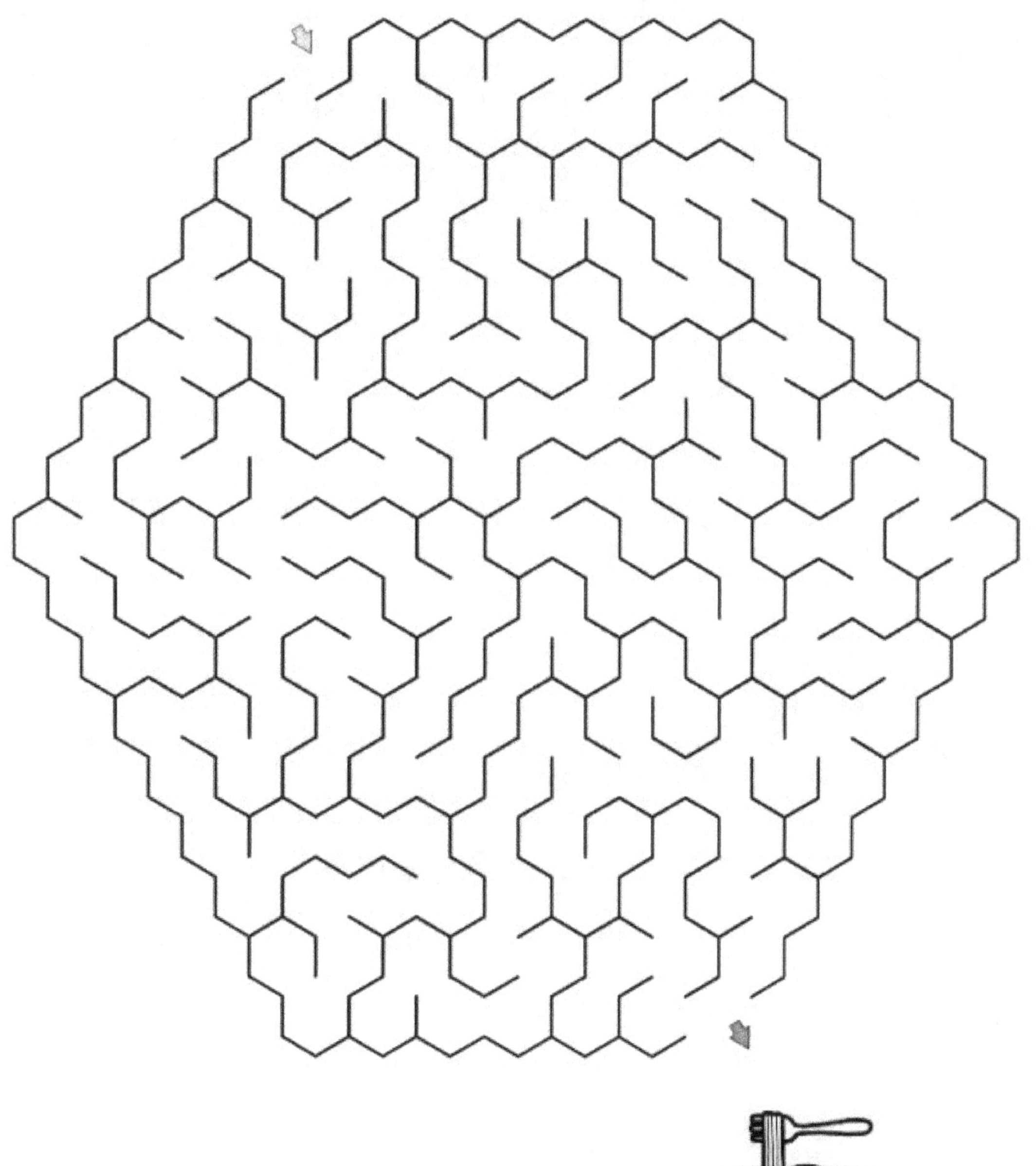

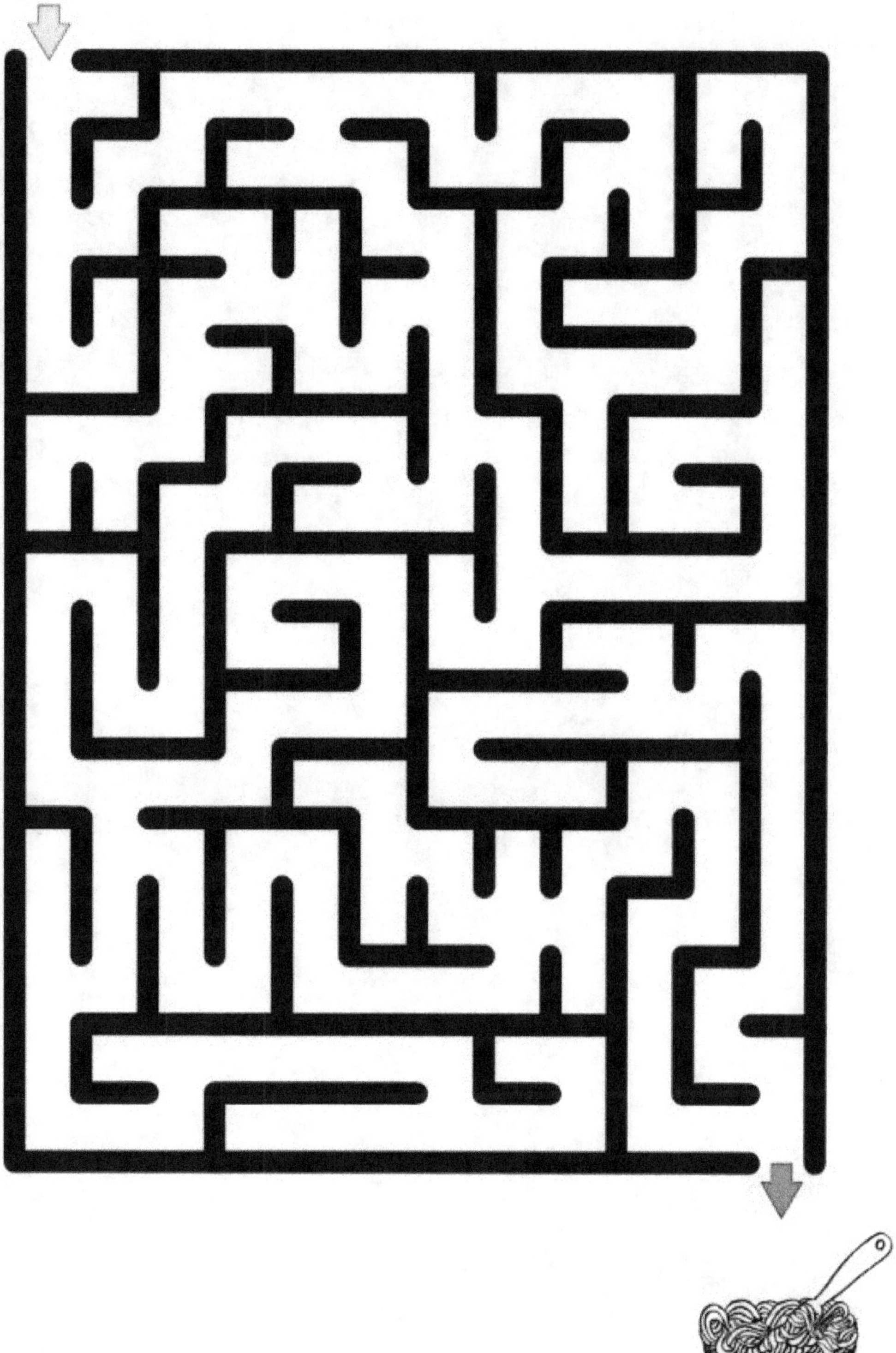

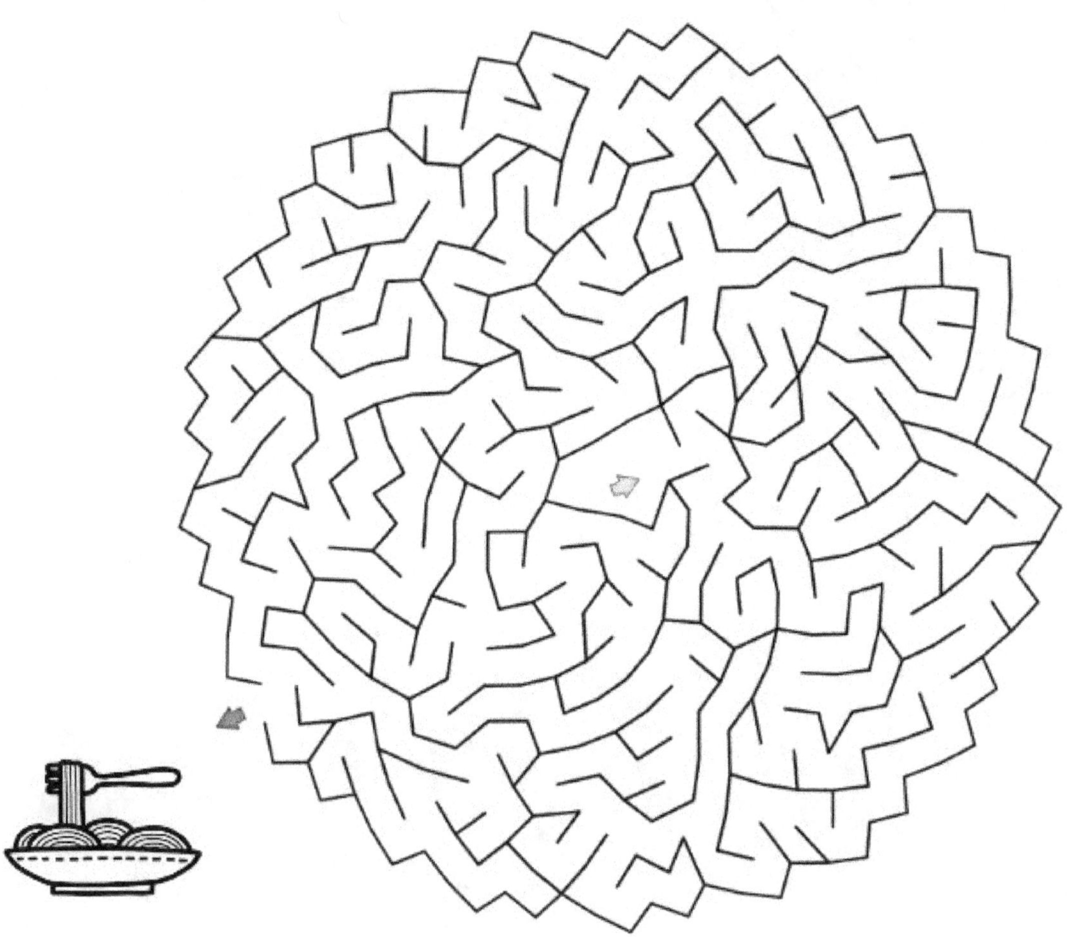

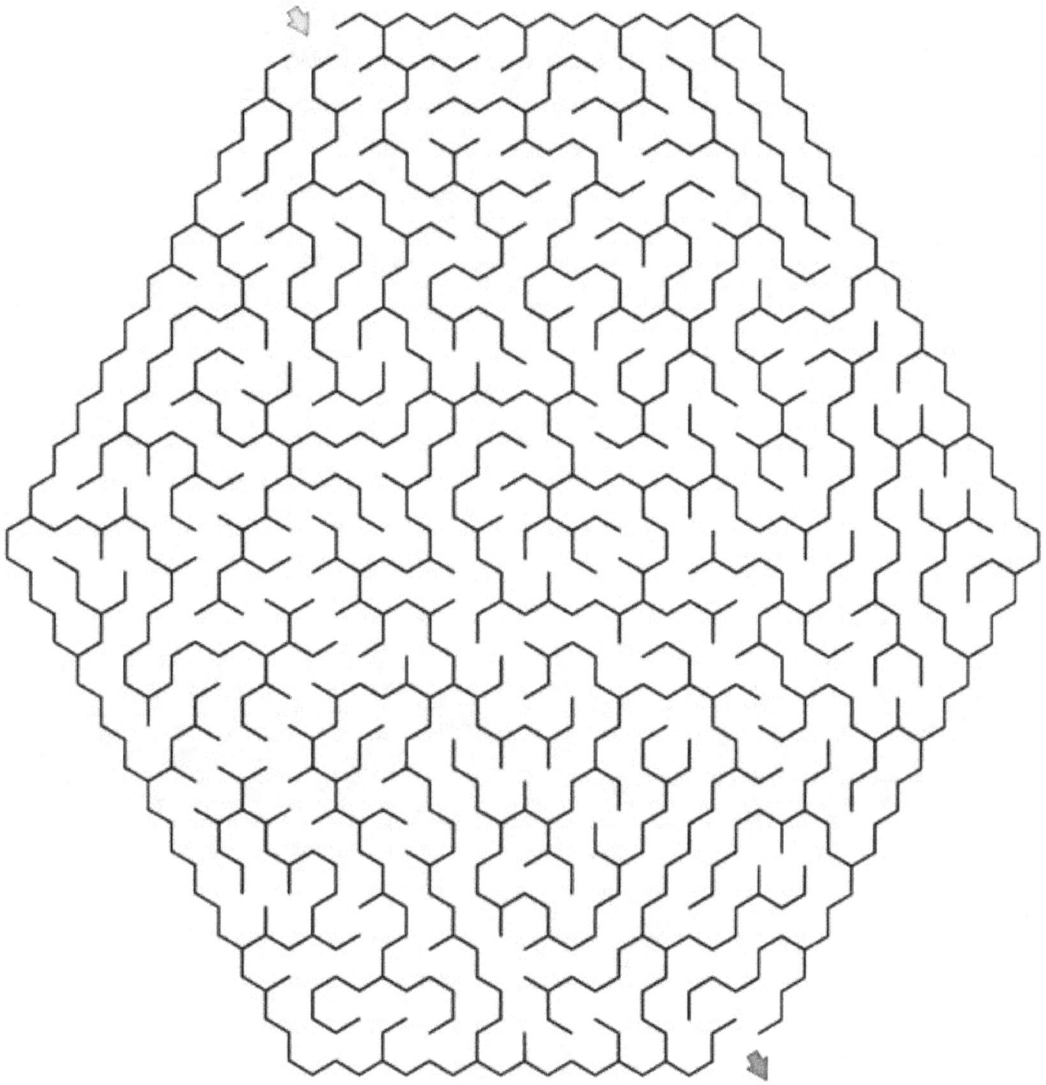

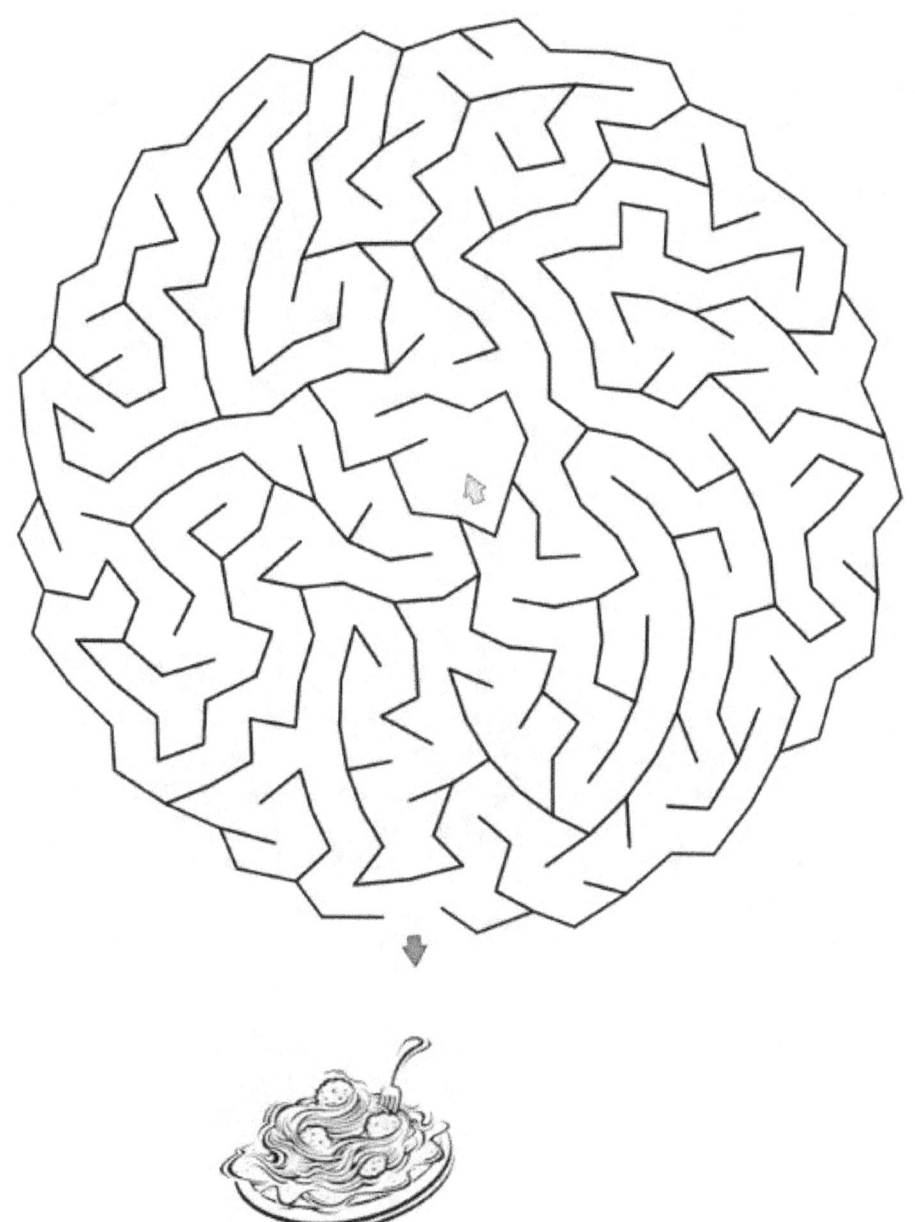

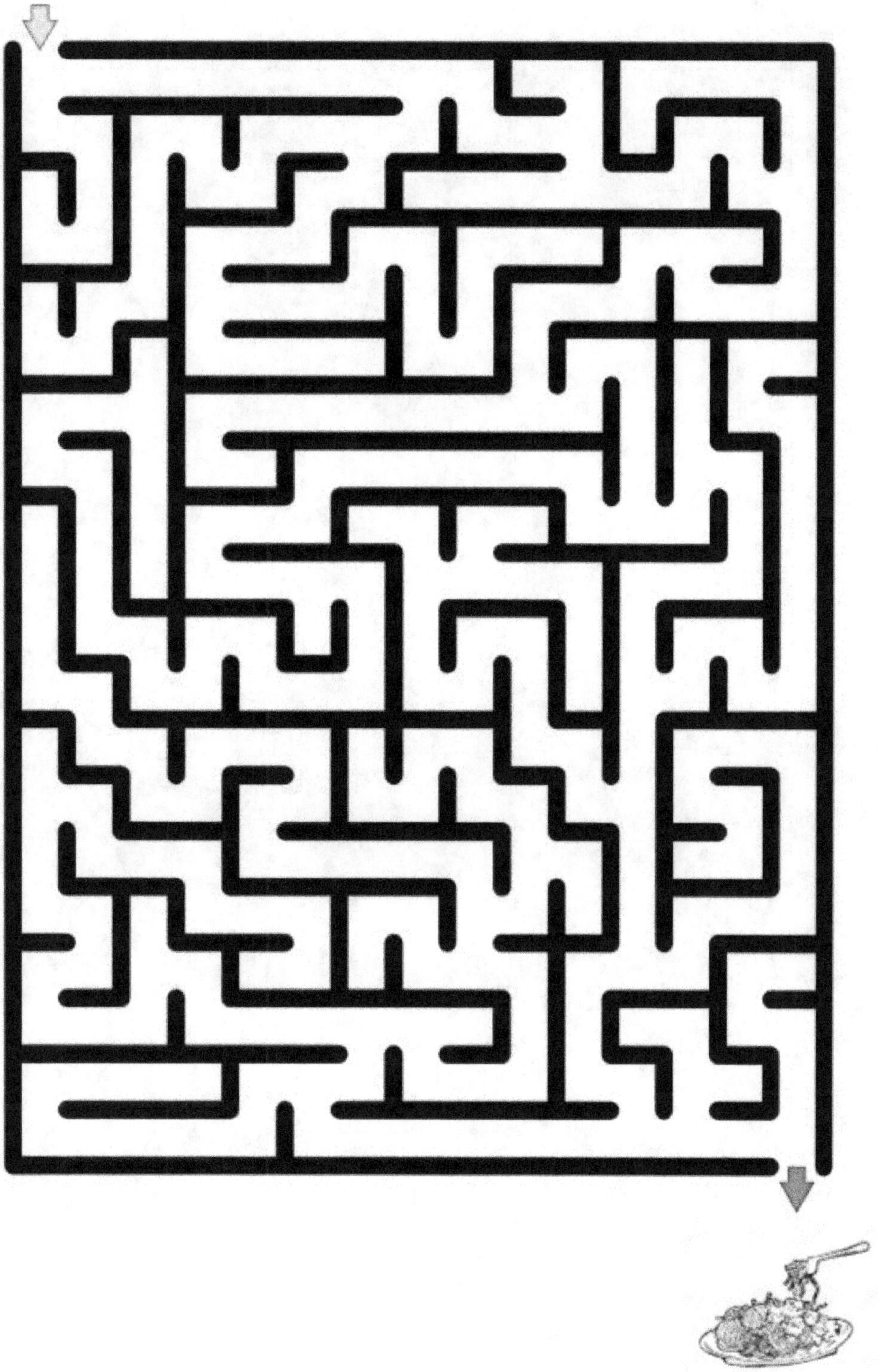

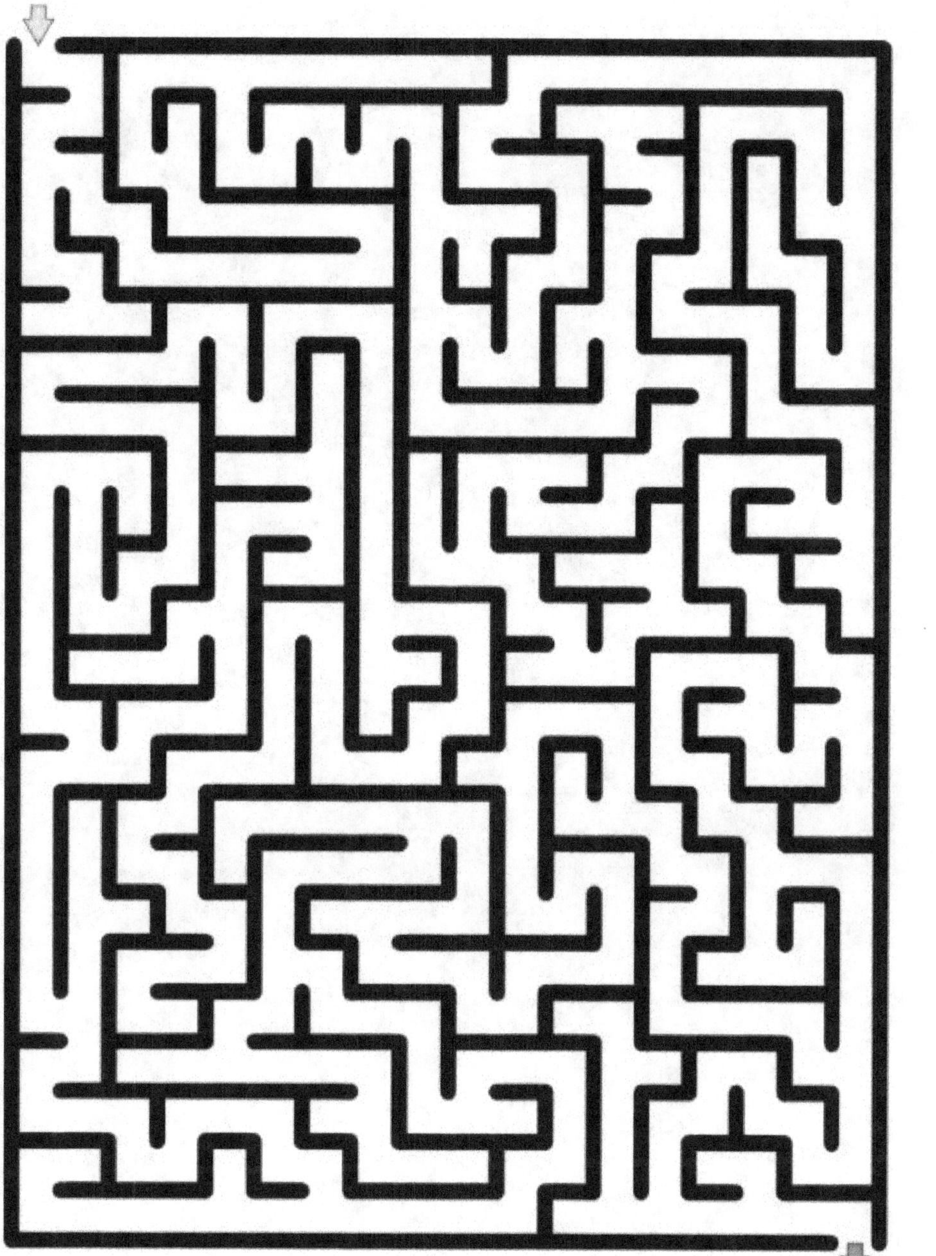

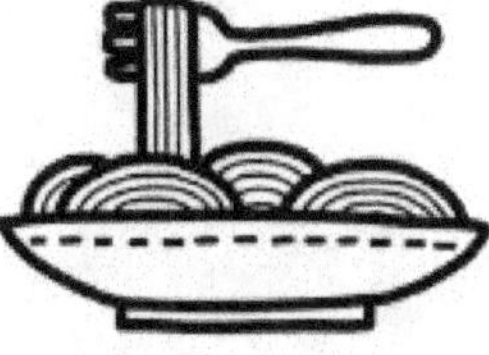

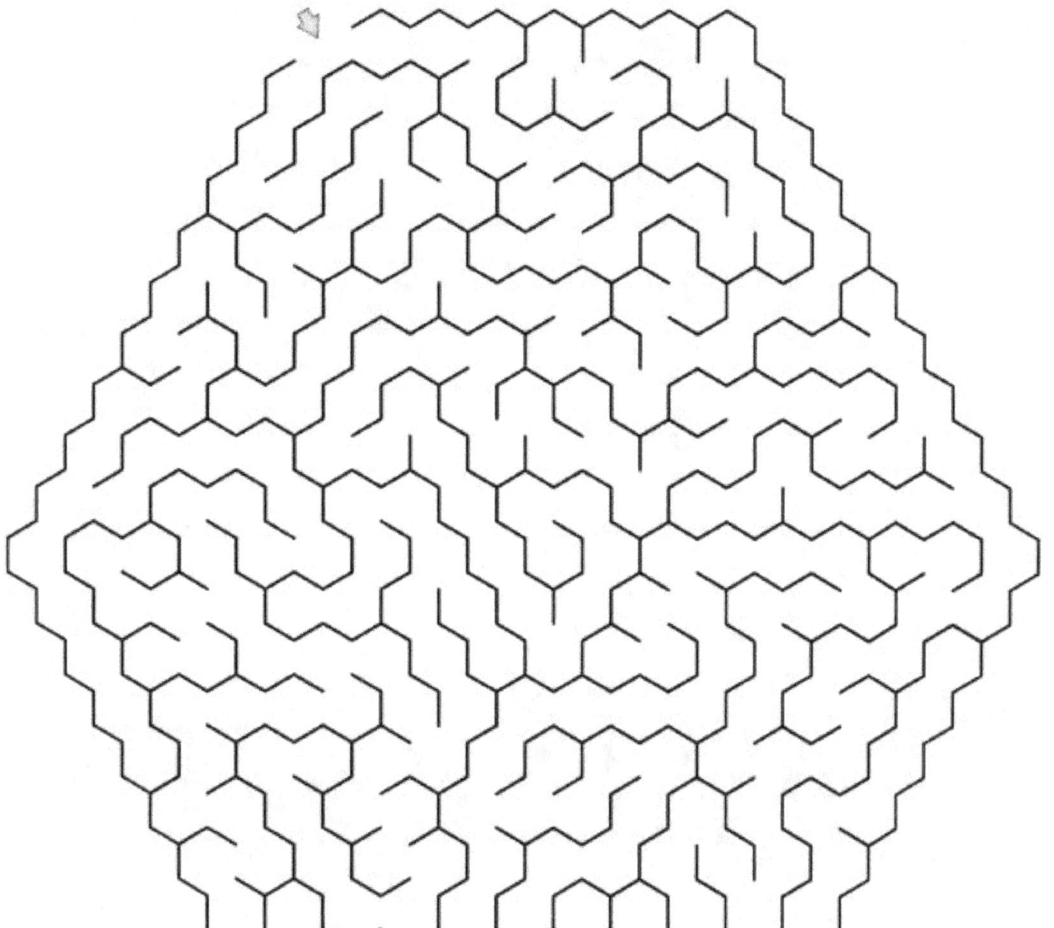

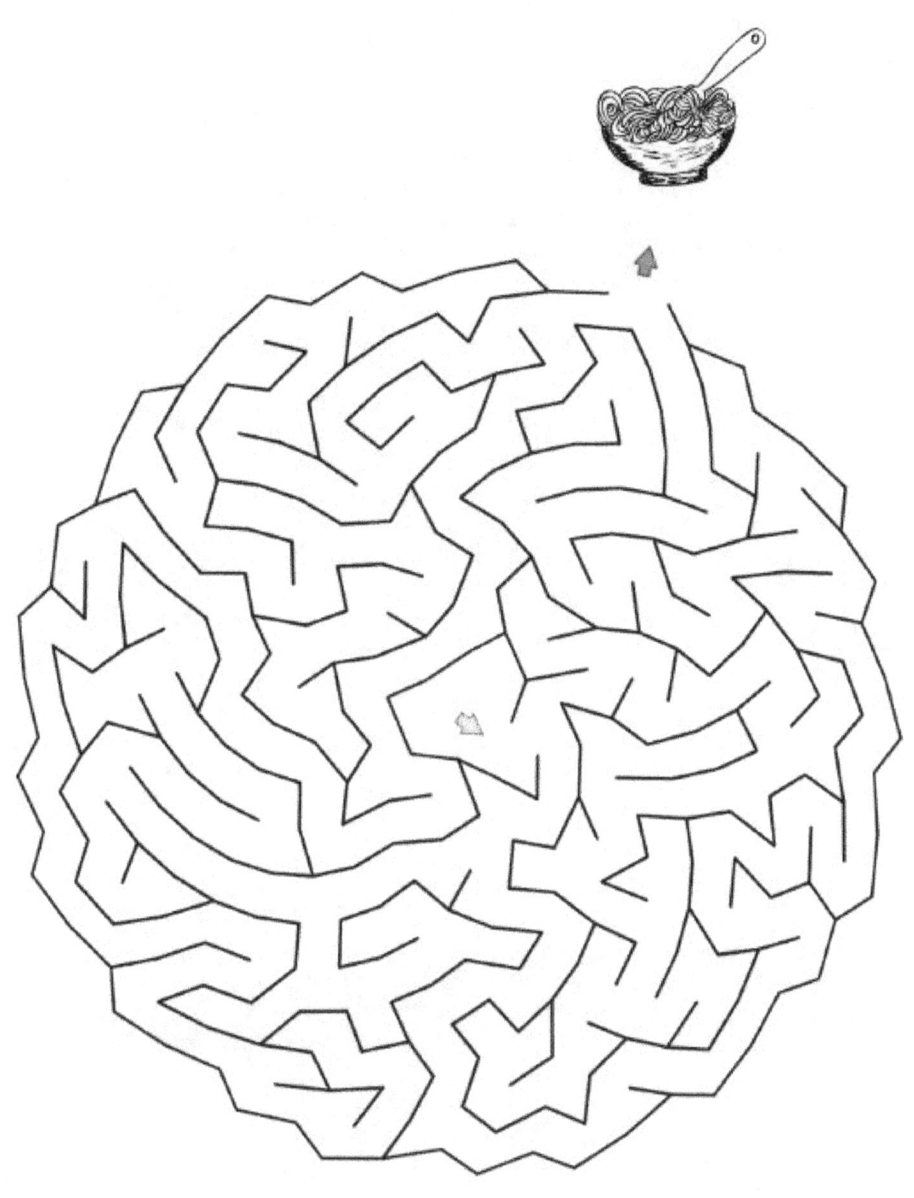

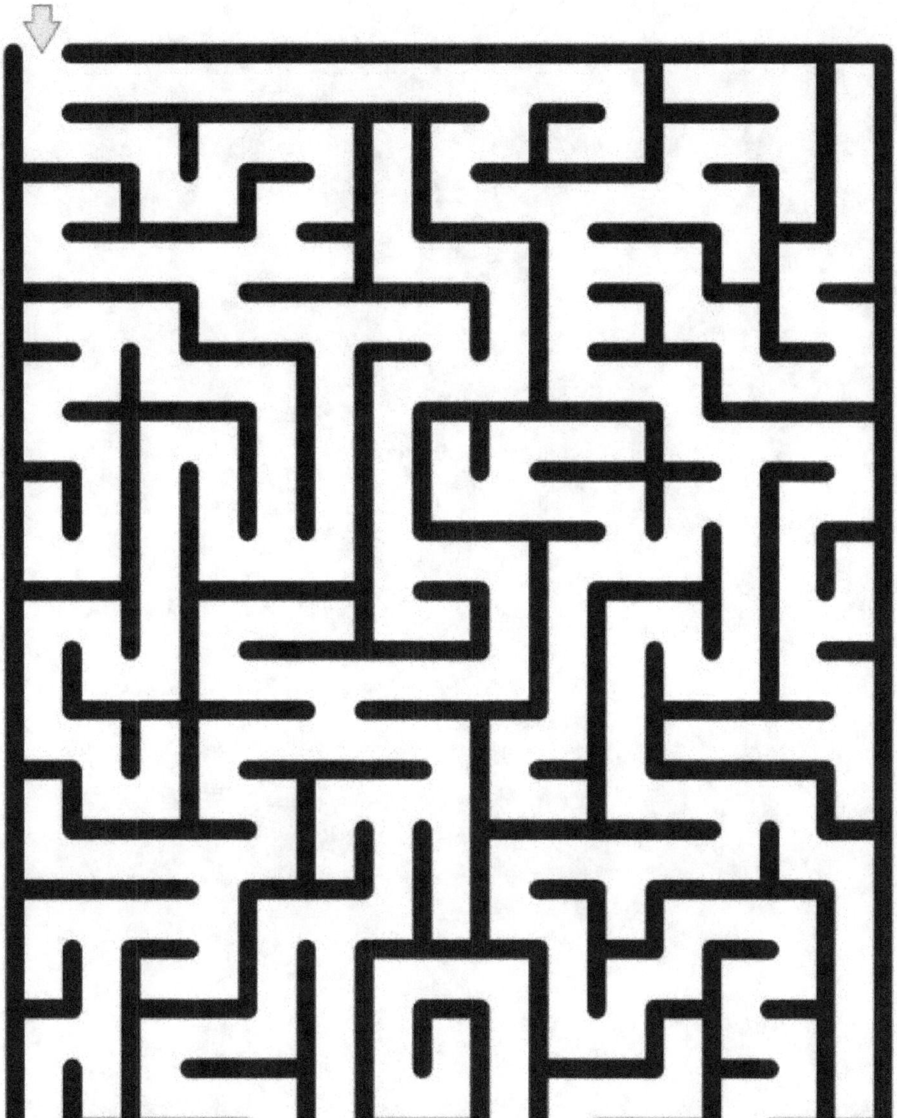